MORNA D. HOOKER

Continuity and Discontinuity

Early Christianity in its Jewish Setting

EPWORTH PRESS

7162 0429 0

First published 1986
by Epworth Press
Room 190, 1 Central Buildings
Westminster, London SW1H 9NR

Printed in Great Britain by
Richard Clay (The Chaucer Press) Ltd
Bungay, Suffolk

65, 695

CONTENTS

PREFACE

These four lectures were delivered as the Sanderson Lectures at the Theological Hall of the Uniting Church in Australia, in Ormond College, Melbourne, during March and April 1986. An earlier vesion of the lectures was given as the James Gray Lectures at Duke University, Durham, North Carolina, in November 1984. My husband and I are grateful to those in Durham and Melbourne who invited us to share for a short time in the life of their institution, and who made us so warmly welcome in each place.

I am grateful, also, to those who have urged me to make these lectures available in print. In response to their request, I am presenting them here almost in the form in which they were delivered, with the minimum of editing, and without annotation, as a foretaste of the book I hope eventually to write.

M.D.H.

I

Understanding the Context

I am quite sure that Australians must get extremely tired of the many jokes about their way of life that depend upon the assumption that those of us who live in the northern hemisphere are normal, and that those living in the Antipodes are odd. Such humour is tedious; nevertheless, jokes often disguise important facts, and it is certainly true that to visitors from the other side of the planet some things do appear strange. For example, Australian seasons are – to my northern way of thinking – back to front, so that when it comes to celebrating the Christian festivals, something very strange indeed takes place; and at this point I really do have to insist that the southern seasons are out of step, since a great deal of the imagery and myth- ology attached to the great festivals of Christmas and Easter belong to their provenance and celebration in the northern hemisphere, and seem quite out of place when the seasons are reversed. Yet it is necessary for me to ask myself whether part of my problem is not due to the fact that for me England – not Australia, and not Palestine – is the norm. It is not only the trappings of Christmas, for example, that belong to a northern winter, but the inter- pretation given to the stories themselves. Men and women of many generations and places have interpreted the events of the gospel in terms of their own experience: over the ages, artists have depicted the Bethlehem manger as though it were a stable of their own period; generations of carol-singers have sung about the 'bleak mid-winter, long ago', because their own experience of Christmas was associated with 'snow on snow', and it is doubtful whether many of them have ever paused to wonder whether water *did* stand 'like stone' in a Palestinian winter; fewer still will have realized that in Palestine winter is the time of renewal and life, and that it is summer that is the season of death.

Partly through ignorance, partly through laziness, we tend to assume that the rest of the world conforms to the corner of it that is familiar to us. Consequently we suffer from culture shock when we visit a country very different from our own for the first time; and even when we are there, we find it impossible to put ourselves into the skin of a man or woman from another culture, impossible to imagine what it is like actually to *be* that person. However hard I may try, I cannot help thinking in terms of my own experience and knowledge; I cannot empty myself of all it means to be 'me', and build up an entirely new set of thoughts. Like a computer, I have been programmed to 'think' in a certain way.

It is inevitable, then, that we should get the men and women of biblical times wrong, for we interpret their words and actions in terms of our own experience. Part of our problem, I suspect, is that the stories and the characters in them are all so familiar. We have been brought up on the Gospel stories, and so we feel we know Peter and Andrew, James and John. But do we? Have you ever tried to imagine what life was really like for them? What, for example, did they eat at meals? – was it always loaves and fishes? Had they all been to school? – if so, what had they learned there? What did they think about all day? What were the talking points in the village? What did they hope for? How did they understand life? What was the framework of their beliefs? And where did Jesus fit into those beliefs?

Now there are certain things we know about the characters in the story. About those four disciples, for example, we know that they were fishermen; we know that they left their fishing nets and accompanied Jesus as he preached throughout Galilee; but where our knowledge runs out, we tend to assimilate their experiences to our own. We have to make an effort to imagine what life must have been like – and we do not have nearly enough information to help us. So we fill out the details in accordance with our cultural preconceptions. And if that happens at a trivial level, in relation to the practicalities of everyday life, it happens much more disturbingly and dangerously at the deeper level of beliefs and ideas. What did Christian faith mean for the earliest believers? How did they interpret the words we read in our Gospels and in Paul's letters? Words and images change their meaning; they take on a different significance, according to the context in which they are used; but assumptions and interests shift too. My attitudes and approaches are governed by my background, my up-bringing, my experience of life; they form the context in which I interpret any statement of faith which I may make. Yours may not be all that different from mine, but different they certainly are; and those of a group of Christians in Russia will be different again.

Now of course there are certain human experiences and emotions which bind us together, whatever our sex or race, and whatever time or place we belong to: but even here there are significant differences. We must all die; but life expectancy here and in Europe is about three times what it was in first-century Palestine. For most of us, death seems a remote prospect, which we must think about one day – until suddenly we realize that we are older than we thought, or some crisis shatters our complacency. In societies where death is a daily threat, attitudes to it must be rather different from our own. Marriage is another

experience common to men and women of all cultures –
but how very differently the marriage rite is handled in
different societies; indeed, we can see radical changes in
the way in which marriage itself is understood taking place
in our own communities. When we read of life and death
and birth and marriage in our biblical texts, we read them
in the light of our own situation; the very fact that these
are universal experiences may hide from us the fact that
our apprehension of them is likely to be very different.

So what of our apprehension of the Christian gospel? I
have begun by spelling out this problem of changing context and interpretation because the topic I wish to deal
with in this series of lectures is one aspect of it. All of us, in
reading the Bible, bring to it a wealth of past experiences
and present concerns, which govern what we hear it saying
to us. We cannot understand its message, except through
the medium of language, symbols and ideas that are familiar to us. But it is equally true that those who wrote it
could only write through the medium of language, symbols
and ideas familiar to them. The Bible can, of course, speak
to men and women of every age without their necessarily
being aware of the significance that the words and images
used by its writers had for them; nor is this to be dismissed
as an 'unscholarly' approach, for at the moment exploring
what the text has to say without asking questions about
the original author's intentions or situation is the latest
scholarly fashion among New Testament exegetes. But if
we wish to explore what our biblical writers meant by
their own words, and if we wish to discover what those for
whom they wrote understood by them, then we must do
our best to comprehend their world, and the background
of ideas against which these documents were written. My
primary concern is thus to examine the setting in which
these books were written – the background of ideas, prob-

lems and controversies which help to explain why the earliest expressions of Christian faith were hammered out in precisely the way in which they were.

Fashions in New Testament studies, as in many other fields, tend to go in cycles – or perhaps it would be fairer to say in spirals, since we never return to precisely the same point. Not so long ago it was fashionable to stress the Greek background to New Testament thought, and to trace the origins of many of its ideas in pagan culture. At present, the emphasis is on its Jewishness – a swing which was given impetus by the discovery of the Qumran texts, and which accelerated with the new scholarly interest in intertestamental literature and rabbinic writings. Now it is probably a mistake to play off 'Greek' against 'Hebrew' as though they were alternatives, and as though Jew and Greek never met. Most of the New Testament writers were Jews, and it would be strange if they did not approach the gospel from a Jewish perspective; all of them wrote in Greek, and therefore had some knowledge of the world of Greek ideas. Moreover, we must not think of 'Greek' and 'Hebrew' ideas as though they were ready-made building-blocks which were simply incorporated into a new structure. My concern is not to argue for one set of ideas over against another; rather it is to explore the formative influence played on the gospel by its Jewish context, to suggest ways in which that context played a significant part in the development of christological statements, and in particular to examine the tensions between the old and new faiths; for that, assuredly, is where belief in Jesus began – within the context of first-century Judaism.

Now of course the New Testament is not one book but many, and we are not, therefore, looking for a uniform situation. Each book was written in a different setting – and even one book may reflect more than one setting. The

7

process of development and change within the Christian tradition goes back to the very earliest days, because the circumstances of the many groups and individuals who received it and passed it on were so very different. The context in which statements are spoken and read affects the shaping of beliefs at a very basic level. Even the simple question 'Who is Jesus?' sounds different if you have never even heard of Jesus: 'Jesus? – Who's he?' Think first of a crowd of Galilean peasants, listening to the teaching of a strange wandering rabbi who has appeared in their village. He tells stories which catch their interest and make them think about God and about his Kingdom. But who *is* this teacher? Do his words have any authority? Should they take any notice? Can he be believed? Move on twenty years, and picture a small group of Christians, meeting together in that same village, reminding one another of the stories Jesus once told them; but now they are no longer simply stories told by a stranger – they are the teaching of the risen Lord, treasured and remembered; the stories take on new meaning as they are retold and applied to their situation. The teacher they once knew has been vindicated by God himself and proclaimed as his anointed Son – certainly his words may be trusted. Move on another twenty years or so, and think of another Christian congregation, partly, perhaps predominantly, Gentile, gathered together in some big Greek or Roman provincial city – listening to those same stories – perhaps being read now, rather than remembered. But how very different those stories sound – no longer addressed to Jewish peasants, being summoned by a Jewish teacher to return to God, but treated as Christian scripture by a group committed to Jesus as Lord. Now his words are regarded as authoritative commands for the life of the community. The search for the authentic words of Jesus has to contend with many difficulties, and at the end of the day, even if we were convinced that we had succeeded in uncovering the *ipsissima verba*, our search would founder at this final hurdle: words take their meaning from the context in which they are spoken and heard.

Even within the New Testament itself, then, we can detect changes in interpretation taking place – the result of changes in situation. And if changes take place within twenty or forty years, and within a few hundred miles of Galilee and Jerusalem, we ought not to be surprised if even greater shifts in understanding take place later.

Yet one of the most important of all changes in perspective is one whose significance has often been overlooked, and that is the transition of the gospel from being a movement within Judaism to the status of a new, independent religion. Because Judaism and Christianity have long been separate entitities, we tend to read the division between the two faiths back to the very beginnings of the Christian church. Yet the truth is that the majority of the first generation of Christians regarded themselves as faithful Jews, and saw their faith in Jesus as the fulfilment of Judaism. Christianity began as a messianic sect within Judaism, and during most of the New Testament period it was still seeking to establish its own identity; the final break between the two faiths more or less coincided with the end of the New Testament period. Our New Testament documents were written by men who were experiencing some stage of that process of rupture – coping with the first pain of rejection by the parent body, learning to live with the growing tensions between ever-diverging communities, or coming to terms with the final break between the two. But those same documents were gathered together to form 'the New Testament' by those of a later generation, who saw themselves as members of a distinct community, now totally severed from Judaism. Thus the writings of the first century AD became the sacred texts of a church which was influenced by ever-growing antisemitism to think of itself as utterly opposed to anything Jewish.

Fashions, I have said, go in cycles, or rather, in spirals. If I stress the importance of the Jewish context for understanding the origins of New Testament Christianity, some of you may think that the spiral has not really taken us much further. But we never return to precisely the same spot. Older biblical exegesis tended to stress the unity of Old and New Testaments, and to play down the tensions; so did the so-called 'biblical theology', which flourished in the 1950s. There was a tendency to treat Judaism simply as the religion of the Old Testament — as incomplete, the preparation for the New Testament, always pointing beyond itself to Christ. Now this is a judgment on the Old Testament which those of us who are Christians may well wish to endorse, because it corresponds with our experience; this is how we read the Old Testament — and, as we shall see, it was how our New Testament authors came to read it. But it is hardly fair to Judaism, and our increased understanding of first-century Jewish belief and practice has led us to recognize that Judaism must be recognized as a faith in its own right. First-century Jews certainly did not regard their religion as incomplete, or as a mere preparation for something better; the Jewish Torah — the Law given to Moses on Mount Sinai — was God's perfect revelation to his people. If we are to understand our New Testament writers, then we must remember that most of them — perhaps all — had been brought up as devout Jews; to their Jewish contemporaries, Judaism was still the norm, Christianity the deviation. It was Christians who began to reinterpret the Old Testament scriptures, and emphasized the element of promise, so that they became a

10

series of pointers to Christ. But we do an injustice to Judaism if we approach it simply from a Christian perspective; nor shall we understand the emergence of Christianity if we treat it in this way.

My concern, then, in this series of lectures, is with the problem of continuity and discontinuity, and with the ways in which the religious ideas of the past were used and refashioned; with the relationship between Christianity and its mother faith, Judaism, and with the links and tensions which held them together, until something snapped and they became independent entities.

Let me draw an analogy which will, I hope, be clear to you all, even though it is taken from the English scene. The position of the early Christians must have been in some ways similar to that of Methodists in eighteenth-century England, where the established religion – the only recognized religion, indeed – was that of the Church of England. Methodism began as a society within the Anglican fold, and for many years prominent Methodists – most notably John Wesley himself – remained loyal members of the Church of England. But gradually they found themselves excluded from the parent body – they opted out, or they were pushed out, as the tensions and differences increased. For a long time, however, individual Methodists continued to worship in the parish church as well as attending Methodist preaching services; their Methodism was complementary to Anglican traditions, not in contradiction with it. Yet tensions there certainly were. This pattern continued even after Methodism had formally broken away from the Anglican Church – in some places until well into the nineteenth century. My own great-great-grandfather, for example, who came of good Anglican stock, but who lived in Cornwall, where Methodism thrived, used to worship in the parish church of St Just-in-

11

Roseland on Sunday mornings, while on Sunday evenings he risked the anger and ridicule of the Rector, when he took his tuning-fork to the Methodist chapel, to 'raise the tunes' for the service there. It is hardly surprising that the break between Anglicans and Methodists finally came about: it proved impossible to go on with a foot in each camp. Methodists were no longer at home in Anglican churches; villages were divided into hostile factions, owing loyalty either to church or chapel, and for many chapel-goers, anything smacking of 'church' was anathema.

Methodists in England are still a small, minority group, and consequently still feel the need to explain themselves. It is true, of course, that increased secularization means that even Anglicans now find themselves belonging to a minority in our community. Nevertheless, membership of the Church of England is still regarded by many as the norm; those who belong to any other Christian community are assumed to be Nonconformists. I have been struck, when visiting America, by the totally different situation there; for in America, where there is no established church, it is not particularly odd to be a Methodist, and no-one there would suppose that they had to explain why they were not an Episcopalian. No analogy is ever perfect, but we may perhaps draw a similar contrast between the position of Jewish Christians in Palestine in the middle of the first century AD, under pressure from their fellow Jews to conform and regarded as the odd ones out, and the situation in the rest of the world at the end of that century, as Christianity spread among Gentiles. For though it remained for centuries a minority religion, it was no longer a sect struggling to find its identity within Judaism, but simply one religion among others: Christians might well be called on to explain why they were Christians – and, indeed, to do so with their lives – but they were no longer seen as Jewish heretics; Christianity had become an independent religion, with its own norms and limits.

Now there are certain very important changes which come about when a community moves from a situation in which it is still within the orbit of the parent community, or separating itself from it, to an independent existence. The metaphor I have just used – 'parent' – gives us the closest analogy. A child leaving home and setting up house for himself or herself, has to adjust to having a new centre in his or her life; the focus of existence changes, as ties with parents are loosened. Independence – whether for an individual, a community, or a country, means a whole change in outlook; this is not necessarily deliberate; if one moves house, the view inevitably changes.

Children tend to be like their parents; they inherit the same genes, and they are subjected to their influence. It would be surprising if Christianity were not in some respects like Judaism, and Methodism like Anglicanism. But when a separation comes about with any degree of animosity, then two factors are likely to militate against these similarities. First of all, one may lose certain emphases which once were taken for granted, precisely because they were provided by the parent body, and are left behind in the move. Take those early Methodists, attending worship at the parish church in the morning, and their own preaching service at night. When the breach came, some Methodist societies deliberately adopted Anglican forms of worship, but others simply continued what had become the distinctively Methodist forms of service. My Cornish ancestors, for example, when they ceased to attend the parish church, substituted another preaching service in place of Morning Prayer. Methodism was thus impoverished, for it gradually lost part of its heritage – the liturgy of the Anglican Church: the two Christian communities inevitably drifted further apart, and tolerance was replaced by animosity.

Something similar may well have happened in the early church. According to Luke, the first Christians in Jerusalem were loyal in their attendance at temple worship; it was natural for them – as pious Jews – to go there to pray. Similarly, Paul used to attend synagogue in the various cities he visited, and preach Christ there, until he was forcibly prevented by his fellow-Jews from doing so. From the Christian side, there was nothing incompatible between Jewish worship and Christian faith, and Jewish worship was the proper context in which to express that faith. But what happened when Christians were barred from Jewish worship? If they were barred from worship in the temple, then they could no longer share in the sacrifices offered there. Now because Christ's death has for centuries been interpreted as the perfect sacrifice, we tend to assume that Christians never took part in Jewish offerings; but certainly Luke portrays Paul as doing so, and Paul himself makes plans in his letters to go to Jerusalem for Pentecost, one of the major Jewish feasts. It is probable that the idea that Christ was the replacement of Jewish sacrifices was worked out as the result of being cut off from those sacrifices, rather than vice versa. Christian Jews were no longer able to worship in the temple, and their initial reaction was probably one of sorrow; but then they would come to terms with the new situation. What need had they to worship in Jerusalem, they asked, when they had the perfect sacrifice in Jesus? Just how many Jews did in fact make the journey to Jerusalem in the middle of the first century AD we do not know, but in theory, at least, the festivals celebrated there lay at the heart of Jewish worship. When Christians abandoned them, this was a major shift in emphasis. Now for two reasons, the differences between Judaism and

Christianity at this point were not as great as they might have been. First, because many Jews outside Palestine never actually made the journey to Jerusalem: for them, the temple was a symbol of God's presence, rather than a place of regular worship; secondly, because in AD 70, the temple itself was destroyed: Jews, like Christians, had to adapt to a religious system without sacrifices, and solved the problem in their own way. But by this stage the break had come, and so the solutions to the problem were different. With the temple destroyed, the Torah was now the only focus of Judaism; for Christianity, both Torah and temple were replaced in a remarkable way by Christ.

More devastating, perhaps, were the results of being barred from worship in the synagogue, for that was where Jewish worship took place locally, week by week, and that was where Jewish Christians, both in Palestine and beyond, had at first continued to worship. For them, being barred from the synagogue would mean not only excommunication but treatment as outcasts from society. Jewish Christians in this situation in Palestine set up their own, rival synagogues: the two groups (orthodox and Christians) differed little, apart from their acceptance or rejection of Jesus as Messiah. In the Diaspora, Christians also found themselves being excluded from the synagogues; they, too, formed their rival gatherings. Though synagogue worship would have exerted some influence on them it is likely that these groups were less influenced by Jewish tradition, more liable to change, than communities living in Palestine. As the Christian communities became predominantly Gentile, so the Jewish presuppositions and ethos weakened – as did the Anglican influence in those early Methodist societies in which few of its members had ever been loyal to the Anglicans.

The other factor which prevents children being like their

15

parents is, of course, the deliberate rebellion of the children: they naturally emphasize those things which make them different – the things which make them themselves. Methodism, searching for its raison d'être, stressed certain specific doctrines; only an outsider would have supposed that this meant that Methodists had abandoned the rest of the Christian faith. When family squabbles arise, they are concerned with points of disagreement; a vast area of agreement is taken for granted. Christianity, growing up within Judaism, took for granted the major tenets of the Jewish faith – its monotheism, its belief in God as Creator, and Lord of history; its conviction that God had revealed himself to Moses and the prophets, and that the scriptures were the witness to this revelation. It was not necessary for Christians, living in a Jewish environment, to spell out these beliefs. If you have ever hunted through the pages of the New Testament for a suitable reading on the theme of creation, or God's holiness, or wondered why there is no appropriate reading for Harvest Festival, you will know what I mean. The disagreement between Jews and Christians centred on the figure of Jesus, and this is reflected in the pages of the New Testament, since its authors were primarily concerned with questions of christology. Jesus was the new factor in the situation: it was he who needed explanation. Inevitably, Christians stressed the importance of Jesus and of response to him. Now I am not saying they were wrong to do so: I *am* saying that if we take note only of the controversies between Jews and Christians, and of the distinctive features which Christian writers felt they had to stress, we shall see things from the wrong perspective; we must not forget the common ground, about which they did not need to argue. But because the New Testament is concerned with working out these new beliefs, its writers tend to concentrate on spelling out the distinctive features

16

which now separated Christians from Jews. Incidentally, that is a process which has been repeated again and again at later stages in the church's history, when emphasis has been laid on particular truths by particular groups – but that is another story. What concerns us now is to recognize that because, from the resurrection onwards, the spotlight has been focussed on Jesus, this has distorted our picture of him – for certainly he was not concerned to proclaim himself – and it has led us also to misunderstand the position of the earliest Christians. We have tended to see both Jesus and the early Christian community out of context. In subsequent lectures we shall be seeing how closely bound up these two questions – the questions of Jesus' identity and of the identity of the community – were. I hope to look at some of the ways in which men and women of the New Testament period set about expressing their experience. Next, I want to explore the pressures which forced Jews and Christians apart and so opened up the gulf between Judaism and Christianity, and at the way in which the differences between the two faiths have been exaggerated in later centuries, because the texts of one period were reinterpreted in terms of the context of a later situation.

II
New Wine

'No one pours new wine into old wineskins; if he does, the wine will burst the skins, and the wine will be wasted, and the skins as well. New wine must be put into fresh wineskins.' Jesus' parable in Mark 2.22 is familiar to us all, but its meaning is by no means as straightforward as it seems at first hearing. Clearly, it suggests the incompatibility of old and new: the new wine will burst the old skins. Moreover, the call for fresh wineskins to hold the new wine implies that the new wine is of value, and must be preserved. But how are we to apply the parable?

The setting of the parable, in all three Synoptic Gospels, is a debate in which Jesus is questioned about the behaviour of his disciples, whose failure to fast is contrasted with the practice of other religious groups among the Jews. The first readers of the Gospels would certainly have seen the relevance of the story to their own situation; for they were coming under attack because they did not conform to the usual understanding of Jewish piety. The reply given here by Jesus to those who challenged *him* suggests that the evangelists intended their readers to conclude that the new wine of the gospel cannot be contained within the confines of Judaism. The disciples of John the Baptist adhered, like the Pharisees, to the old patterns of religion; but the disciples of Jesus belong to a new era, so that the old rules no longer apply.

Yet the loss of the wineskins is apparently regarded by the evangelists as being as much of a disaster as the spillage of the wine: 'the wine will be wasted,' writes Mark, 'and the skins as well.' Matthew spells this out even more clearly, for his version runs: 'New wine must be put into fresh wineskins – that way, both the wine and the skins are preserved.' As for Luke, he is concerned not only for the old wineskins but for the old wine, since he concludes the story with a saying to the effect that no one who has tasted old wine wants to drink new, since the old is better. Connoisseurs of wine might well agree with Luke's assessment, but it is a strangely conservative sentiment to find in Luke's Gospel – so much so that commentators usually explain the statement as an example of irony. And in the context Luke has given it, it is difficult to know how else to explain it; for how could Luke have believed that the old wine of Judaism was preferable to the new wine of Christianity? But though one can understand why someone might want to preserve old wine, it is by no means clear why one should preserve old wineskins. If they were no use for wine, why keep them? Were old wineskins used for some other purpose? Perhaps so, but so far none of the authorities I have consulted has been able to explain to me what this was.

The twin parable with which this one is linked in all three Gospels is even more confused. 'No one sews a piece of unshrunk cloth on to an old garment,' writes Mark; 'if he does, the patch will tear away from it, the new from the old, and make a worse tear.' Matthew's version is almost the same. But what, then, do they suppose one should do? Find an old piece of cloth to patch the old garment? That seems to be the logic of the parable as it stands. Or are they hinting that one should throw the torn garment away and buy a new one altogether? That would fit the conclusion of the other parable, which tells us to put new wine into fresh wineskins. But Mark and Matthew do not mention a new garment – only Luke does that, and he seems to be in a total muddle. 'No one tears a patch out of a new garment,' he writes, 'and puts it on an old one. If he does, then he will tear the new garment, and the piece he has taken from it will not match the old garment.' But if the picture he paints is a ludicrous one, maybe that is the point: it would indeed be absurd to spoil a new garment by cutting a patch out of it. It is clear that Luke believes old and new to be incompatible. But which is better? Old wine is best, he says – and does he perhaps think that an old coat is more comfortable? Yet that hardly accords with Luke's conviction that something new is taking place in Jesus. It must surely be Jews who claim that the old wine is best. Luke himself is certainly not clinging to Judaism and spurning the gospel!

The ambivalent attitude towards what is old which is displayed in the different versions of these two parables reflects an underlying tension which runs throughout much of the New Testament: it is the tension between old and new, between the beliefs and assumptions which the first Christians inherited from the past and the new insights of the gospel, between the framework of ideas which formed part of their heritage and the events which made them think again about their understanding of God and his world. To what extent was the faith of the church new? In what ways was it related to the past? Was the church simply a reform movement within Judaism, patching things up where they had gone wrong? Or must the followers of Jesus abandon the old wineskins of Judaism, the old garment which was past patching? And if so, was there really no hope for the religion they had left? Were the old skins and the old garment of no further value, fit only to be thrown away?

If the way in which the evangelists have handled these parables is confused, it is surely because neither model expresses the whole truth. By the time they were writing, Christianity certainly could not be seen as a mere reform movement within Judaism: the patch had torn away from

23

the old garment, and was no longer part of it. But neither was it a separate garment – a separate movement; for it had begun within Judaism: the wine *had* once been contained in old skins. If the images do not fit very well, then this is because we have here an example of the process we were discussing last time: sayings spoken in one situation are interpreted in a different way when they are heard in another. When Jesus spoke about new wine in old wineskins, and a new patch on an old garment, his words were probably intended as a challenge to his hearers to respond to his new teaching about the Kingdom of God – and as a warning of the changes in outlook which such a response will entail: the new situation demanded new attitudes. By the time the evangelists came to write they perhaps saw new and old as two diametrically opposed systems, for the new was tearing out the old, and Christian discipleship and Judaism now appeared to be incompatible. But they were incompatible precisely because Judaism had rejected Christian claims for Jesus, and the small messianic sect had therefore broken away from the parent body. The different versions of the sayings which the evangelists record witness to the discussion that had gone on in between, as men and women wrestled with the problem of relating old and new.

An interesting variation on the theme of new wine is found in the Fourth Gospel, in the story of the wedding at Cana. The old wine runs out, and Jesus changes water into wine; he does not merely make good the deficit, however, for the wine supplied by Jesus proves to be superior to the old: remarkably, those who taste the new wine discover that though 'the old is good', the new is better. But notice that the water which is miraculously changed is poured into stone jars which were used to hold the water required for Jewish rites of purification. The miracle symbolizes the replacement of Judaism by Christianity, but at the same

24

time reminds us of the link between the two. The old has not been abandoned – it has, as it were, been recycled: the old water of Judaism has not been thrown away, but transformed into the wine of the gospel.

The conviction that something new and decisive took place in Jesus has meant, inevitably, that the differences between old and new have been emphasized, and this has sometimes led to the condemnation and rejection of everything Jewish. But Jesus himself grew up within Judaism, and we certainly cannot understand this teaching if we forget that fact. Interestingly enough, it is Jewish scholars who reminded us of the Jewishness of Jesus: they have pointed to the parallels between Jesus' teaching and that of other Jewish teachers, and have argued that from the very beginning, Christians have misunderstood and distorted his words. We should certainly give heed to what Jewish scholars say, for they are in a better position than Christians to appreciate the Jewish element in Jesus' teaching. But the more they argue in this way, of course, the more they blame the writers of the New Testament for altering his message, and introducing an essentially new religion; the gap between Judaism and Christianity remains as great as ever. The more Jesus is seen as a Jewish prophet or rabbi, the further he himself is removed from the church.

Recent scholarly work on the Gospels has also tended to drive a wedge between Jesus and the church – but at the same time it has separated him from his Jewish contemporaries as well. Perhaps it was inevitable that in trying to discover the historical Jesus, and to reconstruct his teaching, scholars should stress what made his attitudes and teachings unique; after all, it happens all the time, to a lesser extent, with attempts to write biographies of particular individuals, and to assess their achievements. If you want to explain why X or Y was important, you will stress the things

25

which made him or her different from other men and women – that particular combination of qualities and experiences which made each one unique. When this process is applied to Jesus, it tends to leave him high and dry from his contemporaries. It has been pushed to its extreme in recent years in the so-called 'criterion of dissimilarity' which has been used by many New Testament scholars in an attempt to discover the authentic teaching of Jesus. The criterion is based on an assumption of discontinuity, not only between Jesus and Judaism, but between Jesus and the church: the rule it offers us is that we can attribute to Jesus with confidence only that teaching which does not overlap either with the beliefs of contemporary Judaism or with those of the early church. The weakness of the method is immediately apparent, for if it is applied rigorously, it is bound to produce a picture of Jesus which allows him no roots in Judaism, and no influence on the Christian community. But even where the criterion is not applied rigidly, it still tends to stress the differences between Jesus and Judaism on the one hand, and Jesus and the church on the other. The notion of discontinuity is built into the method, and the results are inevitable.

But there are other factors which have led Christians to stress the differences between their own faith and Judaism. I reminded you last time of the fact that because our New Testament documents were written by members of a breakaway sect, they inevitably concentrated on what was new: the texts they wrote were therefore primarily christological. That means that when these texts are read out of their original context – and that context included all that Christians had inherited from Judaism – we lose sight of a large element of continuity precisely because the links which bound these men and women to the past are no longer clear to us; when they are read in a different context, there is inevitably a strong element of dislocation, and the uniqueness of their faith is exaggerated.

Later historical developments have strengthened this tendency. First of all, there is the influence which later enmity between Jews and Christians has had on our thinking. Antisemitism became a pervasive influence, regrettably affecting even Christian scholars. Jews were labelled 'God-killers', and their sufferings were seen as divine punishment; indeed, their corporate guilt was made an excuse for persecution and abuse. The roots of this enmity lie in the New Testament period itself, but later events multiplied the bitterness and hardened the divisions. Read through the Fourth Gospel, and you will find that Jesus' opponents in debate are regularly described as 'the Jews'. Now Jews they certainly were – but so, too, was Jesus, and so were his disciples; it would not have occurred to anyone, during the ministry of Jesus, to label those of his fellow-countrymen who were unresponsive to his message as 'the Jews'. By the time the Fourth Gospel was written, however, Jesus' followers no longer consisted of a small band of Jews; they had been joined by Gentiles – a new religion had emerged, and it cut across racial boundaries. Meanwhile, Jewish Christians found themselves being ostracized by their fellow Jews and expelled from the synagogues, and so had to adjust to being accepted as Jews no longer: thus it was that 'the Jews' became the opposition, and the term came to be used of those who had rejected Jesus, and so – in Christian eyes – had forfeited the claim to be God's people. But in John's day the hostility between the two groups had not yet reached the intense pitch of hatred that characterized later centuries. Moreover, the point at issue between the two groups was still clear: was Jesus, or was he not, what Christians claimed him to be? After centuries of conflict, the real issues tend to become blurred: one is 'Jewish' or 'Christian' by inheritance, environment and culture; just as, in Northern Ireland today, one is either 'Catholic' or 'Protestant', whether one has any Christian belief or not.

The Synoptic Gospels seem to reflect a somewhat earlier situation, for in them we find specific groups being singled out for condemnation; those who oppose Jesus and who reject his teaching and mighty works are Pharisees, scribes, the chief priests and Sadducees; the crowd of ordinary people – the *hoi polloi* – respond with enthusiasm to Jesus, though their enthusiasm runs out at the point of commitment. Now it is undoubtedly true that Jesus met with hostility from groups of his countrymen, and in particular from religious leaders. But what we know about the Pharisees, at least, from sources other than the Gospels, suggests that Jesus' teaching was not so far removed from theirs as we sometimes suppose, and that the blanket condemnation of the 'scribes and Pharisees' as hypocrites may be unjust: there were good, devout Pharisees in the time of Jesus, even among those who did not respond to his teaching. But this question of their response is for the evangelists the significant feature. By the time the Gospels were written, the failure of religious men to respond to Jesus was clear evidence, not simply of indifference, but of culpable blindness. God had spoken through Jesus: God's Spirit had been at work in him; those who did not respond to him were blind and deaf to God's activity – their hearts were hardened. This was a deliberate refusal to obey God: men who claimed to be striving for perfect obedience to God's Law were – in Christian eyes – guilty of rejecting his Messiah. So all Pharisees were lumped together; all were hypocrites, since they claimed to love and serve God, but in fact turned their backs on him.

When we read Matthew 23, for example, we find a swingeing attack on 'scribes and Pharisees', apparently without distinction. 'Woe to you, scribes and Pharisees, hypocrites! because you shut the kingdom of heaven against men ... Woe to you, blind guides, straining out a gnat and swallowing a camel. Woe to you, scribes and Pharisees, hypocrites! for you cleanse the outside of the cup and of the plate, but inside they are full of extortion and rapacity ... Woe to you, scribes and Pharisees, hypocrites! for you are like whitewashed tombs, which outwardly appear beautiful, but within they are full of dead men's bones and all uncleanness. So you also outwardly appear righteous to men, but within you are full of hypocrisy and iniquity. Woe to you, scribes and Pharisees, hypocrites! ... you are sons of those who murdered the prophets. Fill up, then, the measure of your fathers. You serpents, you brood of vipers, how are you to escape being sentenced to hell?' This is pretty vigorous stuff, and no doubt there were some scribes and Pharisees who deserved it – but did they all? It seems unlikely. But just as John condemns all Jews because in his time they were opposed to the Christian community, so the Synoptic writers condemn the scribes and Pharisees because they were the groups who were chiefly concerned to put the Christian heresy down.

Let me make it clear that I am not suggesting that Jesus himself never met with opposition, or that he did not find himself in disagreement with some of the religious leaders of his day. Of course he did; it is simplistic to suppose (as some scholars have occasionally done) that because we can discover a setting for the Gospel stories in the life of the Christian communities – that is, see how the stories were being used and applied in changing situations – that they could not have a setting in the life of Jesus himself. What I *am* saying is that words spoken in one situation can come across very differently when they are heard in another. And, indeed, when words spoken in one situation are 'remembered' in another, they may well be sharpened up – the emphasis subtly changed – by small alterations. In Matthew 23, it may well be that warnings once spoken by Jesus to some of the religious leaders, exposing their hypocrisy and urging them to repent, have become for Matthew uncompromising condemnations of men whose attitudes are implacable, and whose condemnation is certain. And we, reading his presentation of the material nineteen centuries later, assume that it was like that from the beginning. But if we do, then we get Jesus wrong; and we get the early Christian community wrong, too, because we fail to observe one of the formative influences at work on its development – the cut and thrust of debate, of accusation and counter-accusation, between Jews and Christians; or rather, between orthodox Jews and the Christian heretics in their midst.

Consider another example in Matthew of the way in which a change in situation makes words come across very differently, and so exaggerates the differences between Judaism and Christianity; this time, however, the shift is between the evangelist and ourselves, rather than between Jesus and the evangelist. The history of the interpretation of Matthew 5–7 provides a fascinating example of the way in which scripture is expounded in accordance with the situation and presuppositions of the exposition. Is the Sermon intended as a new Law, replacing that on Sinai? As a universal code appropriate for those who believe in the fatherhood of God and the brotherhood of man? Or as an impossible ideal, designed to reduce men and women to their knees in recognition of their sinfulness? Take Matthew out of its original context, and the Sermon can be interpreted in any of these ways – and in many more. But if we try to put ourselves back into the first century, and to imagine the problems and tensions which existed in Matthew's own community, the whole passage looks rather different. One striking feature of the Sermon is the series of antitheses in chapter 5: 'You have heard that it was said of old . . . but I say unto you.' Many an exegete has argued that Jesus (at least as Matthew presents him) is here setting himself over against the Law. But is that so? For in the verses which introduce this section, in 5.17ff. we read: 'Think not that I have come to abolish the Law and the prophets; I have come not to abolish them but to fulfil them. For truly, I say to you, till heaven and earth pass away, not an iota, not a dot, will pass from the Law until all is accomplished.' Unless Matthew is a complete fool, he cannot believe that the sayings which follow are intended to attack the Law.

Here we have a notable example of the tension between old and new – between the revelation of God's will given in the past and the new understanding of that will which had come through Jesus. How does Matthew hold them together? We cannot explore this particular problem in detail, but it is clear that the contrast set out in Matthew 5 is not between the Law given on Sinai and a new Law given by Jesus, but between the partial understanding of the divine will which came through Moses and the fuller revelation which is now given by Jesus. It is not a question of two different laws, but of one reality – the will of God – witnessed to by the Law and the prophets, but now made plain by Jesus. The Law given in Sinai was not wrong – but it was incomplete, and now its completion is here. That is why the words of Jesus 'replace' the words of the Law. But the Law has not been proved wrong by his coming; rather it is proved to be right – fulfilled. And that is why, in turn, the righteousness of Jesus' followers must exceed that of the scribes and the Pharisees, since they are God's people, the true Israel. Matthew 5–7 reflects the pressures on a small community which was being accused of deserting the

31

traditions of the past and abandoning the Law. They rebut the charges and return the attack claiming that *they* are the true inheritors of all the promises of God to his people, and that it is they, rather than the scribes and Pharisees, who are truly obedient to God's will. The antitheses – the contrast between old and new – are wrongly interpreted unless we remember also the continuity between old and new.

Matthew's Gospel appears to have been written in a situation where the debate between Jews and Christians was vigorous and heated. Luke's reflects somewhat different problems; but that does not necessarily mean that we understand him any better! Sometimes, I suspect, our critical analyses lead us astray. One of the most influential books of recent years has been Conzelmann's analysis of Luke's theology; he suggests that Luke divides time into three distinct periods: the period which we would describe as 'BC': the period of Jesus, and the period of the church; the first is covered by the Jewish scriptures, the second by Luke's own Gospel, and the third by his second volume – the Acts of the Apostles. Now Conzelmann may well be right: maybe Luke *does* see history in this way. Nevertheless, I suggest that his thesis has distorted our understanding of what Luke is trying to do. For notice how once again this interpretation has emphasized the gulf between Judaism and Christianity – a double divide, indeed, since Judaism belongs to period one, and Christian faith to period three. Yet one of the remarkable things about Luke's writings is the way in which he takes care to emphasize the *links* between what happened 'BC' and what happened in the birth, life, death and resurrection of Jesus, and between the ministry of Jesus and the life of the Christian church. The first two chapters of Luke's Gospel – which Conzelmann, unfortunately, missed out of his analysis – make it clear that Luke sees the events of the Gospel as the continuation of

God's saving acts in the past; and the opening verses of Acts 1 make it equally clear that he sees the life and work of the church as the continuation of the life and work of Jesus. For Luke, the *links* between old and new are just as important as the division.

And having turned to Acts, it is worth noting another example of the way in which we perhaps misread the tension between Judaism and Christianity and exaggerate the differences between them. In Acts 7, Stephen is accused by the Jews of teaching against the Law and the temple. Commentators often complain that Stephen's speech is irrelevant to the charges brought against him; in fact, it is highly relevant, for what he does is to turn the tables on his accusers: it is they, he declares, who are disobedient to God's commands, delivered on Mount Sinai; it is they who do not realize that the temple is only a symbol of something much greater. The implicit claim in this is that it is Christians who are truly obedient to God's commands, and who worship God as he should be worshipped. Taken out of its context, Stephen's speech does sound like an attack on the Law and the temple; I suggest that we ought rather to understand it as part of an ongoing debate between Jews and Christians as to which of them are truly faithful to God and to all that has been revealed in the past.

It is important to remember that in the earliest period of the church most of the men and women who confessed faith in Christ were Jewish in origin, even though Paul was busy turning the world upside down with his Gentile mission. But what about Paul? If he was indeed the apostle to the Gentiles, do we still have to remember the Jewish context here? Did he not bring in outsiders, converting pagans who had no grounding in Judaism?

Certainly he often addresses his converts as ex-pagans, but no-one who has wrestled with Paul's theology will be in any doubt that it is impossible to understand Paul himself without remembering his Jewish background. Remarkably, he seems often to expect some knowledge of Judaism among his readers, for many of the arguments he uses would have been lost on his readers unless they had some familiarity with Jewish beliefs and modes of argument. Of course, it may be that they *were* lost on his readers, and that it was for this reason that he had such trouble with some of his churches! But certainly those churches included Jewish converts, and it may well be that many of the Gentiles were former God-fearers, with a high awareness of Jewish beliefs. But whatever their background, the gospel which Paul proclaimed to them concerned the God of Abraham and of Moses, and the question of the place of Christians – whether Jewish or Gentile – within the people of God was of vital importance to them all.

Not suprisingly, then, we can easily get Paul wrong, too. Let us take a well-known verse from Galatians – Galatians 3.13: 'Christ redeemed us from the curse of the Law, having become a curse for us – for it is written, "Cursed be every one who hangs on a tree".' When that verse is read to a Christian congregation on Sunday, how do they understand it? Naturally, they identify themselves with Paul's experience: Christ has redeemed us – us Christians.

But you will notice that Paul is writing specifically about being redeemed from the curse of the Law, and a couple of verses earlier he has told us that it is those who rely on the works of the Law who are under this curse. Who is it that relies on the works of the Law? – why, Jews, of course. And if we start to look at the context of this passage, we will find Paul making a distinction between Jews and Gentiles. 'We ourselves,' he says in 2.15, 'are Jews by birth and not Gentile sinners.' So when Paul writes, 'Christ redeemed us from the curse of the Law,' he means, 'us Jews'. It is an idea

34

that he spells out in the next chapter: 'God sent his Son, born under the Law, to redeem those who were under the Law.'

But, you will say, the whole point of Paul's argument in Galatians 3–4 is surely to show that there is no distinction between Jew and Gentile in Christ – and so it is. But in Paul's day, the experience of conversion meant different things for Jew and Gentile. We Jews, he says, have been redeemed from the curse of the Law; as for Gentiles, they have received the promise made to Abraham that men and women of every nation should be blessed. We Jews have 'come of age', and been acknowledged as God's sons – only to discover that Gentiles, too, have received God's Spirit, and are as much God's children as we are. And though Paul argues that for Christians to put themselves under the Law is as much bondage to alien powers as was the service of pagan deities, there is no doubt that the experience of conversion to Christianity must have been very different for pious Jews on the one hand, and Galatian Gentiles on the other. But what happens when Paul's words are read in a community whose members were brought up neither as Jews nor in a pagan environment – a community such as our own? In a later century, Gentile Christians read Paul's words, 'Christ redeemed us from the curse of the Law', and applied them to themselves. They assumed that when Paul wrote 'we' and 'us' he meant 'we Christians' – and that was not entirely surprising, since sometimes that is precisely what Paul *does* mean! But not always. And when, as often, he means 'we Jews', or 'we Jewish Christians', then we Gentile Christians of a later generation have certainly reinterpreted his meaning, when we apply his words to ourselves.

Once again, I am not suggesting that later Christians have been wrong to reinterpret Paul's words in this way. I am simply pointing to the fact that words spoken or written in one context sound different in another. The fact that God still speaks through those words, even when they are transplanted to a new situation and reapplied, is an interesting demonstration of the role which scripture plays in every generation. How this happens is a matter of hermeneutics, but we must confine ourselves to matters of historical investigation. My concern is to remind you that it may be precisely in applying the scriptures to ourselves today that we distort their original significance. If we want to understand what Paul originally meant by his claim that he had been 'redeemed from the curse of the Law', then we must endeavour to put ourselves back into his shoes, and to understand what was going on in the communities to whom he was writing.

Now what Paul said about the Law – not only in Galatians, but more particularly in Romans – did have a major influence on the development of later Christian theology, more especially through the influence of Luther. This is not the time or place to discuss the rights and wrongs of Lutheran theology, but you will see at once that Luther was doing precisely what I am suggesting took place. Luther was no Jew; he was no first-generation Christian; he had never been 'under the Law', and had therefore not been redeemed from its curse – not, at least, in the sense that Paul himself had understood those words. Luther applied Paul's teaching to his own situation: his experience of mediaeval Catholicism was of a religious system which made impossible demands of him, and so induced an intolerable burden of sin. For Luther, the works of the Law were no longer simply the demands of the Jewish Law, but his own futile attempts to earn salvation by his own efforts, and he interpreted Paul's experience in that light.

The Lutheran contrast between Law and grace picks up an antithesis which is present in Paul's own writings. But the contexts in which the two theological debates took place were quite different. Luther was concerned with his own personal salvation, and with the abuses of mediaeval Catholicism, which 'offered' salvation in return for 'merits'; Paul was concerned with the terms on which Gentiles were to be admitted to the Christian community. In the past, God's people had been singled out as the nation which had accepted his Law and promised to live by it. Could Christians now claim to belong to his people *without* accepting that Law? The answer given by experience was 'Yes', because God's Spirit had already been poured out on uncircumcised Gentile converts, who had thus already been marked out as God's children. In spite of similarities in argument and vocabulary, and in spite of their fundamental agreement in seeing the gospel as sheer grace, the problems confronting Paul and Luther were not the same, and neither were their answers. But because Luther's interpretation has been so formative for later Protestant theology, and because Paul's particular problem is so remote from our own, whereas Luther's individualistic interpretation of Paul's teaching – like that of Augustine before him – finds echoes in our own experience, Protestant Christians have tended to read Paul through Lutheran eyes ever since. We have tended to assume that Paul shared Luther's personal agonies concerning his own salvation, and we have tended to attribute to first-century Judaism some of the failings of fifteenth-century Christianity. The result, I believe, is that we have distorted Paul's understanding of the Jewish Law; by concentrating on the negative statements in Paul about Judaism, and about the past, we have tended to exaggerate the gulf between the old religion and the new. Moreover, we have tended to overlook what was for Paul a monumental problem: if Jews were now spurning the gospel and Gentiles were flocking in, what had gone wrong with God's plan?

Why had the people whom God had been preparing for a thousand years stumbled at the last fence? Was Israel no longer God's chosen people? Had his purpose failed? These were burning questions for Paul – but in a later period they were no longer important. Paul was seen simply as the great apostle to the Gentiles; because Christianity became predominantly Gentile, it seemed as though God had abandoned Israel, and as though Gentiles had simply taken the place of Jews in God's plan. But that was certainly *not* how Paul saw it! Of course he himself contrasted the old and the new, law and gospel, Moses and Christ. But he maintained to the end that God had been at work in the past; that the Law itself had been given by God, and that God had not abandoned his people. He saw a continuity between his past beliefs and his present faith, as well as discontinuity. In stressing the new at the expense of the old, later Christians lost sight of something that our New Testament authors were maintaining.

III
Old Wineskins

In my last lecture, I pointed to some of the pressures which had led to an undue emphasis on the discontinuity between old and new, and on the division between Judaism and Christianity. The divisions and hatred of later ages have, I suggested, distorted our understanding of what was going on in the New Testament period, when the break between the two religions was not yet complete. But, of course, that is only part of the picture: indeed, you may well have thought that I was exaggerating the dislocation that took place when Christianity was severed from Judaism. For we are surely all aware that Christianity began within the fold of Judaism. Are not the links between old and new obvious, symbolized in the binding together of Old and New Testament in one volume? Have not Christians acknowledged their indebtedness to Judaism, even while they have stressed their opposition to it as a religious system? Perhaps; but the question I want to raise today is this: are the ways in which we normally trace continuity between old and new in line with those of our New Testament authors? I have suggested that we may have misunderstood the element of discontinuity in the New Testament because we read the writings in it from a later perspective; we have emphasized what divided old and new and forgotten what they held in common. I now want to suggest that even when we have been aware of the links between old and new, we have often misunderstood the way in which the New Testament authors themselves traced continuity with the past. And once again, I must stress that I am making no judgment

41

about the rightness or wrongness of what we have done: Christians are bound to interpret and express the truth in terms appropriate to their own situation, but if we want to understand what the New Testament writers were doing, then we must certainly attempt to see things from their viewpoint, rather than from our own. Let us look, then, at a couple of the ways in which the notion of continuity between old and new is often traced, for I suspect that our perspective may have led us to view the links between past and present in a rather different light from that in which the first Christians saw them.

I suppose that the commonest and most obvious way of tracing the continuity between old and new, between Judaism and Christianity, is to talk in terms of promise and fulfilment: the period of the Old Testament is seen in terms of promise, the gospel as the fulfilment of that promise. The clearest way of demonstrating this theme of promise and fulfilment is the quotation of Old Testament texts, which match up with events in the life of Jesus, and with the experience of the early Christian community. But notice how different this theme of promise-and-fulfilment looks to us, surveying the biblical story from a distance, than to those who were involved in it. Christians have pored over the scriptures, both old and new, for centuries: they have traced the story of redemption, 'from its first beginnings' to its conclusion in the life, death and resurrection of Christ. And when you know the end of the story, then earlier events begin to fall into place. Anyone who enjoys a good detective story knows that the author will have scattered clues throughout the pages of the book – often apparently trivial or incidental happenings – which suddenly appear significant when Hercule Poirot or Miss Marple or whoever it is starts putting two and two together; the pattern of events becomes clear only when the mystery is cleared up. When we talk about Jesus being seen as the fulfilment of promises made in the Old Testament, we tend to think of the fulfilment of specific prophecies about future events; and we tend to assume that these 'prophecies' were clear and well-known – that the promises had been set out, and that the whole Jewish nation had precise expectations for the future. In fact, of course, Old Testament prophecies about the future tend to be somewhat general in character. Moreover, to judge from the evidence of the New Testament, it seems that the first Christians may have seen things from a different angle. For they, we must remember, are taking part in the story: they are present at the dénouement, when the detective patiently unravels the evidence, and shows how all the clues point to one person. It is at that moment that the penny drops, and one suddenly says 'So that's what so-and-so meant!' When they claimed that Jesus was the fulfilment of the prophets, they were beginning from their experience of him – from their knowledge of his words, actions, death and resurrection – and from their faith in him, and suddenly, old familiar words began to take on new meaning. In other words, they did not begin with predictions and promises, or with clear expectations about future events and say, 'Yes, Jesus fits the bill'; the disciples did not go down a messianic check-list, ticking off the items one by one: they began with Jesus, and discovered clues in the Old Testament which they had not suspected. So it was not so much a matter of prophecies finding their fulfilment, as that the hopes, ideas and events of the past fell into a new pattern and took on new significance.

Now, of course, if you decide to reread your detective story, it will, unless you have a very short memory, be a very different experience from the first time round: you will not lie in bed reading till the small hours in order to find out what happens, because you know already. And you will find yourself reading the earlier chapters in a different way, too: this time, you will notice important clues, which had not seemed all that significant the first time you read them. And if you pore over your book for years, as Christians have done with the Bible, then you will find that the clues leap from the page, and you will wonder how you ever missed them the first time round.

At this point, my analogy breaks down, for I do not want to suggest that God is the archetypal detective-story writer, deliberately concealing clues in the pages of the Old Testament. I want to go no further than suggesting that the first Christians were rather like detectives, working backwards from the scene of a crime, and asking questions which would explain it – but in this case, they work back, not from a crime, but from their experience of the life, death and resurrection of Jesus. And naturally, in trying to understand and explain these events, they looked in their holy books – which is why our model of promise-and-fulfilment is not entirely satisfactory: for it was more a case of experiencing the fulfilment, and *then* discovering the promises! Things began to fall into place, and a pattern emerged. They had not realized what they were looking for, until it arrived.

Let me give you an example of the kind of thing I mean. Every year, in England, just before Christmas, the BBC can be guaranteed to broadcast a performance of Handel's *Messiah* – probably by the Huddersfield Choral Society, but if not, by some other great choir; the occasion has become as much part of the Christmas tradition as the Service of Nine Lessons and Carols from King's College, Cambridge. Now there is a sense in which we have been brainwashed by Handel – though, to be fair, his libretto only does in music what the evangelists do in story, and what painters and poets have done in art and literature. He offers a picture of Jesus which consists largely of Old Testament texts – those

Old Testament passages which Christians have discovered to match up to later events and experiences: 'Behold, a virgin shall conceive'; 'He was despised and rejected'. And the result is that Christians have tended to assume that in first-century Palestine there were clear expectations about a future Messiah, about who he would be and what he would do. It is assumed that these Old Testament passages already had their place in that picture. In fact, all the evidence points the other way: of course there were hopes, of course there were speculations; but the hopes were many and varied, and the expectations by no means clear. There was no ready-made list of proof-texts awaiting fulfilment. As for the death and resurrection of Jesus, here was something totally out of line with any expectations that first-century Jews might have held for any future Messiah. These events sent Jesus' followers scurrying to their scriptures: how were they to be explained? They looked there for illumination, and they found it – sometimes in what seem to twentieth-century biblical scholars to be most unlikely places. But those Old Testament passages were pieces of the jig-saw which clicked into place *after* the event – and there had not been a copy of the picture on the box to guide them. Most of the texts which the church took over as 'messianic prophecies' were not messianic at all, nor were they 'prophecies' in the way in which that word is usually understood; but from the earliest days, Christians found themselves explaining events by showing how they were 'in accordance' with scripture. Sometimes the appeal was a general one: things had taken place 'in accordance with the scriptures': 'Christ died for our sins', writes Paul, 'according to the scriptures'. Usually, however, the appeal was to specific proof-texts. When that was done, they would either quote a particular passage directly, or weave the Old Testament passage into their own narrative. We can see good examples of these two approaches if we compare the first two chapters of Matthew's Gospel with the first two chapters of Luke. Both evangelists are telling the story of Jesus' birth; both are concerned to show how the events they describe mark Jesus out as the one in whom God is at work, and both appeal to scripture in support of their claims. But Matthew quotes passages from the prophets, introducing each one with the declaration that the various events he describes took place in order to fulfil the prophet's words, whereas Luke tells the story of Jesus' birth in language which is soaked in the vocabulary and style of the Septuagint, and expects his readers to pick up the allusions and to understand that his story is a continuation of the story of salvation recorded in what we call the Old Testament. If their stories about the birth of Jesus are so different, it may be partly because of the different ways in which they have traced this theme of fulfilment.

Whatever method these writers chose, they assumed that the scriptures they appealed to were the authoritative witness to God's purpose, and the record of the way in which he had spoken to his people. And, of course, the Jewish scriptures included not only the prophets, but other writings and, most important of all, the Law. Now since the Law is central to Judaism, we ought to expect the earliest Christians to appeal to the Law as well as to prophets and psalms, but so influenced are we by the antithesis between Law and gospel in later theology that we sometimes do not notice what is going on, Yet one element, at least, in the picture, is their conviction that Jesus was the fulfilment, not just of the prophets, but of the Law also. It is of course true that the evangelists show Jesus in constant conflict with those who were the official guardians of the Law; but the point at issue is usually the interpretation of the Law, rather than the Law itself. The Law itself is taken as given — literally, since it was God-given — and the incidents frequently end with a demonstration that Jesus' own teaching is in accord with that of Moses, while his opponents are shown to be disloyal. We can find examples of this kind of argument in all the Gospels. Here is just one example, from the Fourth Gospel. In chapter 5 Jesus is accused of breaking the Law by healing on the Sabbath, and Jesus replies by turning the accusation around: it is the Jews who fail to keep the Law. The climax comes at the end of the chapter, when Jesus says: 'Do not think it is I who will accuse you to the Father; it is Moses who will accuse you, in whom you have hoped; for if you had believed Moses, you would have believed me, since he wrote about me. But if you do not believe what he wrote, how will you believe my words?'

As for Paul, whom we think of as the great opponent of law, he, too, assumes that Moses wrote about Christ. Indeed, it is precisely when he is concerned to demonstrate the inability of the Law to save that he peppers his pages with quotations from the Law. He, too, uses Moses as a witness to support his case, and to undermine that of his opponents. Like Jesus, Paul is accused of teaching and doing what is contrary to the Law, and he indignantly rejects the charge. 'Do we overthrow the Law by faith?' he asks; 'God forbid! We uphold the Law' (Romans 3.31). Nevertheless, one cannot help but feel that those who wrote the books which tradition attributed to Moses would have been somewhat surprised by the way in which Paul interpreted their words. If Paul found new meanings in old words, he was only using the methods of biblical exegesis which were common among Jewish scholars at the time, but he certainly applied those methods with startling results. Take, for example, Romans 10, where Paul quotes a passage from Deuteronomy 30 about the word which is 'very near you . . . in your mouth and in your heart'. What is this word? In Deuteronomy it is clear that the word is the word of the

Law, but Paul reinterprets the 'word in your mouth' as the word of confession – 'Jesus is the Lord' – and the 'word in your heart' as belief that Jesus has been raised from the dead. The word of the Law has been replaced by the word of faith: Paul has, in effect, made a bold take-over for his opponents' text, and used it to back his own argument. He does the same thing with that famous verse from Habakkuk about the righteous living by faith, for in Jewish exegesis it had been interpreted as meaning that the righteous lived by faithfulness to God's Law. One could hardly describe this interpretation of Old Testament texts in terms of promise and fulfilment; rather is it a case of hidden meanings which leap to life in the light of fresh revelation.

So far I have been talking rather generally about promise and fulfilment, without mentioning one particular aspect of it which is usually central in any discussion about the question 'Who is Jesus?' – namely, the use of the so-called messianic titles. Here, too, I suspect that we have got things badly out of focus, because once again we have looked at the Old Testament with the benefit of hindsight. Let us go back to Handel's *Messiah*. Strictly speaking, the word 'messiah' is an adjective, not a title – though it could, of course, be used with the definite article, and so become a title. But when and where was the title so used? Not, surprisingly, in the Old Testament, where the word 'messiah' is used either of the present king or his heir, and not of some future ruler in the distant future; and surprisingly rarely in Jewish writings contemporary with the New Testament. Now of course there are references to people in the past who have been 'messiah', that is anointed by God for some specific task, and there are hopes of future figures, who will be commissioned for similar tasks; and among the various hopes there was certainly the hope that, when Israel's fortunes were reversed, a descendant of David would again sit on the throne and rule the nation in peace. But it seems very unlikely that the streets of first-century Jerusalem were buzzing with the kind of messianic expectation which we have often supposed to be prevalent or that the Jews of that period had a kind of 'identikit' picture of *the* Messiah in their minds, made up of features drawn from various Old Testament texts. It is *Christians* who have drawn up that picture, beginning from their conviction that Jesus was indeed anointed by God, and then discovering in the Jewish scriptures a wealth of appropriate descriptions. What has happened, then, is that we have defined the term 'Messiah' through our experience of Jesus. Christians have worked backwards from Jesus, and found those Old Testament passages which fitted the reality. In doing so, they were stressing the continuity of God's activity in the past and in the present, and their conviction that Jesus was the fulfilment of past promises.

In trying to sum up who Jesus is, Christians have tended to use a whole series of titles, for what better way is there of expressing who he is and what he does? Titles are convenient shorthand. John Newton's hymn is a good example:

> Jesus, my Shepherd, Brother, Friend,
> My Prophet, Priest, and King.
> My Lord, my Life, my Way, my End,
> Accept the praise I bring.

The New Testament is full of such titles – Messiah, Son of God, Lord, and so on. So that when New Testament scholars have discussed the christology of the New Testament, they have tended to use the titles of Jesus as the framework of their discussion. They have looked at the way in which these terms are used in the New Testament, and they have explored their background in the Old Testament and intertestamental literature. Now I am not for a moment denying that these terms have a background in Judaism — indeed, I would want to stress its importance — but I am suggesting that this whole approach may have things out of focus for two reasons. First, because it has concentrated on the titles at the expense of *other* ways of exploring the significance of who Jesus is, forgetting that titles are only a convenient form of shorthand, and that our Gospels, for example, use stories far more often than titles as ways of expressing the truth about Jesus. Having myself written two books about the titles of Jesus, it is only proper that I should point out the dangers of this approach! Secondly, scholarly concentration on titles has perhaps distorted our understanding of what was happening because it has tended to assume that the titles used of Jesus already existed — as titles — before Christians took them over. In fact, it is more likely that some of these terms *became* titles through being applied to Jesus. 'The Son of Man' is a good example. For years, many New Testament scholars have tended to assume that this was a well-known title in first-century Judaism for an expected future heavenly redeemer, who would put things to rights and introduce the messianic era. The evidence for such a belief has now crumbled, and more and more scholars are coming to acknowledge that there was no such hope and no such title. If Jesus himself used the term, it was not because he wished to claim some well-known messianic office or status; for whatever reason — and the reasons suggested are many and varied — he used the term in speaking of what he conceived to be his mission. It was only later that the phrase, now linked in people's minds with Jesus alone, inevitably became a title. Just as the term 'Messiah' was defined through the experience men and women had of Jesus, so the phrase 'the Son of Man' took on a new meaning through that same experience.

Looking back on the writings of what we call the Old

and New Testaments, we naturally tend to trace the links between the two by beginning at the beginning. Trained as we are in historical criticism, familiar with notions of evolution, we explore the growth of this or that idea and trace the development of doctrines, the origin of hopes which find their fulfilment in later events. Of course that is how we see it, because we stand outside the biblical story, and we see it as a whole. But if we see things from our perspective, so, too, did the New Testament authors see things from theirs. Since they were involved in the story they naturally saw it from a very different angle from those who look at it from outside. Later Christian writers may have seen the biblical story as a long line, stretching from creation to redemption, but these first Christians were conscious of living at the climax of history. Our attempts to sum up what we call 'biblical theology' always work forwards, from the earliest period to the later. But our New Testament writers were working backwards, from the present to the past, and they attempted to explain what Jesus had done and who he was, what had happened to him and what was now happening to *them*, by looking back at the traditions of what God had done in the past. We trace continuity from past to present and on into the future; for them, the thrust came out of their present experience, making them look back at the past. So they traced their experience back into the past, and attempted to show how what had happened in Jesus was grounded in the past. It is notable that if we compare the very different ways in which the four evangelists begin their Gospels, we discover that they all emphasize, in their opening pages, that the story of Jesus can be understood only when it is seen in relation to God's activity in the past. Mark begins with a quotation from the Old Testament: if you want to understand the significance of this story, he says, you must remember the words of the prophets. Matthew, as we have already seen, emphasizes the same theme – but first he traces Jesus' descent back through David to Abraham, because Jesus brings the fulfilment of promises made to God's people in the past. Luke tells the story of Jesus' birth in ways which make anyone familiar with the Old Testament think at once of similar stories and psalms there. John shows how what happens in Jesus had its origins at the very beginning of time: 'In the beginning was the word . . .' For all four, the gospel was the continuation and culmination of God's activity as recorded in scripture. They *began* with their experience of Christ, and looked *back*, into the past, in order to explain that experience.

Although our model of promise and fulfilment appears to link past and present, I suggest that it has in fact, paradoxically, contributed to the *division* between the two, because Christians have tended to emphasize the *contrast* between the period of unfulfilled hopes on the one hand and the time of salvation on the other. Awareness of the early church's apocalyptic hope has perhaps also contributed to this gulf, for we have been very much aware of its forward-looking concern and expectation for the future, and possibly less aware of its concern to link all that happened with their experience of God in the past. In fact, of course, they looked in both directions, for they were at that point which Paul described as the ends of the ages – the overlapping of past and future; they were at the centre of an explosion which was to change things in a way they did not at first suspect. But perhaps we have misunderstood their future-looking expectation also, for one of the changes in perspective between their situation and ours seems to me to be precisely the different ways in which they saw and we see these overlapping ages. For us, it is a straightforward matter of past and future, BC and AD, the period of early Judaism and the rise of Christianity. But they saw these two ages, not as balancing each other, but as totally different in kind; the first Christians stood within the present age; but what was bursting in upon them was the age to come – not simply another period in human history, but the irruption of God's Kingdom into this world. Yet that new age was still only at the stage of bursting in; it was not yet fully here; they were still living in this world – what they *looked* for was a transcendent kingdom. From their perspective, what they were claiming about Jesus was the climax of the past, as well as the foundation of the future.

Even a slight change in perspective can make a great difference to the way in which you see the view. You can stand next to me on a mountain and still not see the church spire I am pointing to if a tree happens to obstruct your view. As we look back on the first century, we tend to talk about the birth of the church, the beginnings of Christianity, and so on; the first generation of Christians would not even have understood the terms we are using. *We* emphasize the notion of something new starting; *they* were witnessing the end of an era and waiting for the new one to begin, even if they were already experiencing some of the spin-off of the future. They saw all things drawing to a close; they certainly were not expecting what happened – the rise of Christianity. So it is that we misunderstand what was going on. Let me give an example. Have you noticed how New Testament scholars have had an obsession recently with the notion of heresy? It began with the Colossians; for a long time it has been assumed that the Epistle to the Colossians was written to deal with some kind of heresy at Colossae. But recently, heresy seems to have broken out all over the place; Paul apparently never put pen to paper, except to put other people right when they had got things wrong. Even Mark's Gospel is said to have been written to deal with a false christology. Now of course the term 'heresy' is an obvious anachronism at this early period; but is not the idea of false christologies equally anachronistic? Are we not using the wrong model? Heresy, false teaching – call it what you will – suggests that Christianity is the norm, and these other teachings are deviants. But is it not much more likely that the basic debate going on at this period is with Judaism? If so, then it is the Christian gospel itself which is the 'heresy' – the deviant.

We need to remember that in its earliest, formative years, the Christian community was working out its understanding of the gospel within the context of Judaism. I should like to pick up my earlier analogy with the position of the early Methodists within the Church of England, and see if that helps us to understand how things developed. We could, of course, equally well use one of a whole series of examples, from the Protestant Reformation down to the latest charismatic community in Africa, but we will stay with Methodism. We have here a religious movement which begins life as a small society within a much larger body, and which eventually separates from the parent body and becomes independent. What are the characteristics of such a sect? We notice that its earliest members insist on their loyalty to the parent body: they are members of the Church of England, and what they believe and teach is in accordance with the doctrines of that church. They rebut accusations of heresy and contravention of the rules, and insist that they are faithful to the traditions of the past; the charges of heresy and disloyalty are turned round upon their accusers. But in time, the new movement attracts to itself large numbers of men and women who have no sense of loyalty to the parent body, and who are not steeped in its teachings and doctrines. At the same time, fundamental doctrinal differences begin to emerge, though each side claims to have the support of God. The split is inevitable; Methodism becomes an independent church, with its own traditions and its own standards, against which heresies are judged. And before very long, the whole process begins all over again, with a split between two groups, each of which claims to be the authentic Methodist community.

If we now try to put ourselves back into a first-century Jewish environment, we will have some idea of the tensions at work in the early Christian communities, as they tried to establish their own identity. These tensions centred on two questions. The first concerned the gospel: what exactly was the message they proclaimed, and how did it relate to everything they had inherited from the past? Since the gospel focused on Jesus, and what God had done through him, this first question could just as well be summed up by asking 'Who was Jesus? How did he fit into the divine scheme?' The second concerned the communities themselves; were they Jewish heretics, as their enemies claimed? Or were they faithful to Judaism, as many of them maintained? Were the Gentiles among them imposters, as orthodox Jews believed? Or were they in fact the founders of a new religion? The problems, in other words, were problems of identity: the identity of the body we call the Christian church, and the identity of the man who had set the new movement rolling.

You will have noticed that, though I began this lecture by looking at christology, I appear to have wandered off into a discussion of the community. This is no accident. The questions about the identity of Jesus and the identity of his followers are firmly bound up together. The answers you give to one determine the answers to the other. Let us try for a moment to put ourselves back into the situation of one of the very first groups of Christian disciples, as they met together in Jerusalem, or in Galilee, or perhaps down on the coast, at Caesarea or Joppa. How did they see Jesus? Of course we do not have any documents from this period, so we must not be too dogmatic, but some things at least are clear. First of all, Jesus was 'a man approved by God ... through whom God had been at work'. This belief had been confirmed by the resurrection, by which God had, as it were, shown his hand; in being raised from the dead, Jesus had received the sign of divine approval and had been proclaimed as Christ, as Lord, as Son of God. The various titles now being given to him show the various attempts that were being made to express in words their belief in what had taken place. But however stunningly new this experience might be, it was seen as a continuation of their previous beliefs and experience. The God who had been at work through Jesus was the God of their forefathers, Abraham, Isaac and Jacob; everything that had happened in Galilee and Jerusalem could be explained as being in accord with the scriptures. The events which they experienced were understood as the fulfilment of past promises.

How, then, did this community see itself? Not, at first, as a separate body, but as a group of loyal members of the Jewish community. How, after all, should they react to the conviction that God had been at work among his people except by renewed obedience to God's commands, and new zeal in singing his praises? The conviction that Jesus was God's anointed one did not, at first, cause his followers to abandon the religion and customs of their fathers: like Methodist societies within the Anglican church, Christians at first appeared to be just another Jewish party.

But very quickly, problems arose. Other Jews began to exclude Christians from their synagogues: each party protested loyalty to the God of their fathers, and each claimed that it was truly God's people, Israel. Worse problems still arose when Gentiles started flocking into the church. Here was a paradox indeed, for uncircumcised Gentiles were claiming to be members of the true Israel, and telling Jews that they had been excluded. Men and women were flocking into the Kingdom of God from the east and west, and sitting down at the banquet, but those who had originally been invited had declined to come. The break was inevitable. The Christian church became a separate entity – the third race, over against Jews and Gentiles. The break meant an immense shift in how Christians saw themselves; it also had a profound influence on how they saw Jesus. For the terms and titles they had used, the language and imagery, were transferred into a new setting, no longer predominantly Jewish. No longer are we dealing with a group of Christian believers who see both Jesus, and themselves, within the setting of Judaism; we are dealing with the Christian church, worshipping Jesus as Lord. It is the pressures which led to that break which I want to examine in my final lecture.

IV

The Wineskins Burst

When I came to write this fourth lecture, and was looking for something to write at the top of the page, I was very tempted to entitle it 'Cuckoo in the Nest'. In the end I abandoned this idea, partly because a cuckoo in a nest made of discarded wineskins seemed a hopelessly mixed metaphor, but more importantly because I realized that a cuckoo was precisely the wrong image for what I have been trying to say about the origins of Christianity. It is true, of course, that a religious movement which began within the Jewish nest soon laid claim to that nest, and saw itself as having replaced Judaism. But cuckoos are intruders, with no lawful claims to the territory they usurp, whereas Christianity claimed from the very beginning to be the authentic offspring of Judaism. First-century Christians certainly did not see themselves as usurpers, but as God's true people, and the rightful inheritors of the promises and privileges given to Israel. I had to reject my cuckoo image, because whatever tensions there were between Judaism and Christianity arose primarily from inside the family. The biblical image is much more apt: it was a case of new wine fermenting and bursting the old bottles in which it had been stored.

It seems clear that what triggered off these crucial changes was the vital question regarding the place of Gentiles in the Christian community. Where and when this first arose we do not know, but certainly it was a central issue for Paul – and no wonder, since he believed himself to have been called to be the apostle to the Gentiles. It is something of a paradox that Paul should have been the one to see the issues so clearly and to take the stance he did, for by birth and upbringing, education and outlook, Paul was thoroughly Jewish. He was, he tells us in Philippians, of Jewish race, a Hebrew of Hebrews – a phrase which may perhaps refer to his language; he belonged to the tribe of Benjamin, had been circumcised on the eighth day in accordance with the requirements of the Law, and was a rigorist in his attitude to the Law, belonging to the party of Pharisees; he had kept the Law perfectly, without the slightest slip; his zeal had been demonstrated in his persecution of the Christian church. He goes on to say that all these things, which he had once considered his pride and joy, he now regards as worthless compared with what had been given to him in Christ. There could apparently be no clearer example of discontinuity – of a man abandoning one set of religious presuppositions and attitudes in exchange for another – especially when we read the passage in the context of the whole chapter, in which Paul launches a bitter attack on those who parade what Judaism had to offer. If we want to know where Christ fits into the divine scheme, the answer seems to be that he has replaced the Law. How is one saved? Not through obedience to the Law, but by faith in Christ. How can one achieve righteousness? Not through keeping the Law, but by union with Christ. What should now govern the believer's way of life? Not the commands of the Law, but the love of Christ. Who are God's people? Not those who obey the Law, but those who are in Christ.

You will notice that in posing the question about where Christ fits into the divine scheme, we have once again found ourselves posing questions concerning the nature of the community which believes in him. And one of the reasons why these two questions are so firmly linked together is that it was precisely the Law which distinguished Israel, God's chosen people, from all other nations. If the Law has been replaced by Christ, then what happens to this fence, which marks off God's people from all others? It is broken down. God's people consist now of those who are in Christ.

What was it that led Paul to see Christ and Law as contrary forces, pulling in opposite directions? Strangely, he never explains. Perhaps it was his own experience. After all, as a persecutor of the church he had certainly seen belief in Christ as contrary to the Law – and he had given his whole-hearted allegiance, first to the Law, then to Christ. Perhaps it was the crucifixion, which he describes as a stumbling-block to faith, for in Galatians 3 he quotes the text from Deuteronomy which declares that any malefactor who is hung on a tree is under the curse of God; it must have been one of Paul's favourite texts in his pre-Christian days. But if God had raised Christ from the dead, what became of the Law which had pronounced him accursed, and in whose name Paul had persecuted his followers? It was devotion to the Law which had led Paul into what he now regards as heinous sin; it was no wonder that Paul came to regard rightousness according to the Law as worthless.

Who, then, is Jesus? And who are the people who believe in him? Let us take one of his letters – the one to the Galatians – and see what he says. The titles Paul uses for Jesus – the shorthand summaries of faith – are the familiar ones: Christ, Son of God, Lord. As for his followers, they are God's people, the true sons of Abraham, and so the inheritors of all God's promises. But is not something rather strange going on here? For if Jesus is Son of God, then he is Son of the God who revealed himself to Moses in the Law on Mount Sinai; and if Christians are children of Abraham, then this means that God has ratified the covenant which he made with Abraham – a covenant described in one of the books of the Law ascribed to Moses. We do not have to pursue any of Paul's theological arguments for long to

63

realize that it is based on his understanding of the scriptures, and that is certainly true in Galatians: one text after another is hurled into the argument. So is not Paul wanting to eat his cake and have it? Can he really appeal to the Law in order to attack it?

I suggested in an earlier lecture that Paul does this precisely because he sees the Law as a witness to Christ. In other words, the model of Paul as an example of total discontinuity which we suggested just now will not do. For all Paul's scathing attack on those who attempt to make themselves righteous by obeying the Law, and for all his denigration of things past in comparison with what has happened in Christ, Paul does not deny that the Law is holy and God-given and has a role in God's plan. Indeed, how could he? For Paul is a Jew, and in becoming a Christian he does not abandon his belief that God has revealed himself in the past. God is consistent; he does not make mistakes; he does not change his mind. An outsider like Marcion might come to the conclusion that the God of the Old Testament was a false God, and not the Father of our Lord Jesus Christ, but that is far from Paul's understanding of the situation. He does not deny that God spoke to men and women in the past, or that he called Israel to be his people; though he castigates those who rely on the Law and on circumcision, he does not deny that God gave the Law to his people through Moses, or that circumcision was the seal of his covenant with Abraham. Paul's problem was the problem with which we have been concerned throughout these lectures – the problem of holding together old and new, of reconciling his belief in the validity of God's revelation to his people in the past with the conviction that God was now at work in Christ. Paul's solution was to look again at his understanding of the Law, and to come up with a totally new explanation of its role. It had, he explains, been a temporary measure, and its regulations had kept God's people in restraint until the time of promise arrived. The promises went back to the time before the Law had ever been given, Abraham had believed those promises, and now they were fulfilled in Christ. Once again, we tend to misunderstand what is going on because we read Paul's solution to the problem, and assume that this is where he began. We assume that Paul first grew dissatisfied with the Law, because he could not keep it, and then found the way out of his dilemma in the salvation he found in Christ. That may be an evangelical experience, but there is no evidence that it was Paul's – indeed, the New Testament evidence is unanimous that Paul first found salvation in Christ, and then – inevitably – realized the inadequacies of the Law. It was a question of beginning from the new experience and asking questions about the old assumptions; of trying to fit Jesus into the beliefs he already had, and finding that he had to adjust those beliefs. Paul worked backwards from his present experience, and read scripture in a new light; and scripture, in turn, provided the key for understanding the present. At the same time it validated the gospel by demonstrating that what happened in Jesus was in line with God's activity in the past.

The conclusion of these arguments was inevitable: on the one hand, the Law witnesses to Christ; on the other, Christ replaces the Law; therefore Christ must be greater than the Law. For why bother to replace old with new unless the new is superior? 'How obvious!' you may say: 'of course Christ is superior to the Law.' But was it immediately obvious to Paul and his contemporaries? For the Law of the Lord was perfect; it was God's self-revelation to man, and even Moses had simply been the one through whom God gave the Law to Israel. God might send prophets and kings to his people, but they would not be greater than the Law. But now God's rightousness is revealed in Christ, and he has taken over many of the Law's functions: the Law has proved to have built-in obsolescence. Great as it is, Christ is greater, and to that extent the Law is denigrated. Anyone who has ever seen a TV commercial knows that the latest improved version of any soap powder now on sale washes whiter than the version we were using last week; this is of course remarkable, since for years we have been assured that the original could not be bettered. What seemed to us, in our ignorance, to be perfect, now bears testimony to the superior quality of the product which replaces it. The Law, which had once been seen as the embodiment of God's self-revelation and of his will for mankind, gives way to Christ, and plays a subsidiary role as witness to his superiority: it was a bold conclusion for those who had been brought up within the Jewish faith.

One of the passages where Paul spells these ideas out is II Corinthians 3. Paul is here comparing his ministry as Christ's apostle with that of Moses – another bold thing to do, since he claims that his own ministry is superior! The chapter is basically a piece of biblical exegesis, in which Paul expounds part of Exodus 33 and 34. The story tells how Moses received the Law from God on Sinai and caught a glimpse of God's glory, as a result of which he himself reflected the divine glory; but Moses' glory faded, for it was only temporary, and it belonged to an imperfect dispensation – that of the Law – which brought death. By contrast, Paul's own face had been set aglow with a permanent glory, a glory which Christians have seen revealed in the person of Christ. Paul does not deny glory to the Law, for it was the revelation of God to his people: but when we compare the Law with Christ, then we see that its glory is only temporary, fading, partial; the glory seen in Christ is the embodiment of divine self-revelation. Instead of a copy, we now have the original.

Is it any wonder, then, that Paul and his followers begin to think of Christ in words and images which they had once used in speaking of the Law? Jewish books of wisdom had described wisdom as the emanation of God's glory, the reflection of his eternal light, the mirror of his power, the image of his goodness; as the master workman through whom God had created the world, the blueprint of creation. And where was wisdom to be found, except in the Law? But now Christ is identified with wisdom, and seen as the image of God and the source of glory.

> He is the image of the invisible God,
>   the firstborn of all creation,
> For in him all things were created,
>   in the heavens and on the earth,
> visible and invisible . . .
>   all things were created through him and by him.
> He was before all things,
>   and all things cohere in him.

So Colossians 1, and even more striking are the opening lines of the Epistle to the Hebrews, by an unknown author who is concerned to show how old and new are related to each other: 'At many times and in many ways in the past God has spoken to our fathers through the prophets; but now in these last days he has spoken to us through a Son . . .'

Here we have a straightforward comparison between prophets on the one hand, and the Son on the other – with the obvious implications that the Son is superior. But notice how he goes on: '. . . a Son whom he appointed heir of all things, through whom also he made the universe. He is the effulgence of God's glory, and the expression of his being, sustaining the universe by his powerful word . . .' The language is the language used of wisdom, who expresses God's will; but now wisdom is embodied, not in the Law but in the Son.

And of course we find similar ideas in that most famous of all passages, John 1, where John speaks of the Word by whom all things were made, of the Word which became flesh, and of the glory which he reveals; like Paul, John picks up the story of Exodus 33 and 34, and contrasts the Law given through Moses with the grace and truth – the fullness of God – embodied in Jesus, whose glory is the glory of God himself.

I have suggested already that too much time has perhaps been spent looking at the titles given to Jesus, and not enough time looking at other ways of expressing who he is and what he does. These passages demonstrate one very interesting way, for they are all concerned with the relationship of Jesus to Judaism. Where did Jesus fit in to the religious beliefs which these writers have inherited? How are they to hold together the conviction that God had spoken to men and women in the past with their new experience of his self-revelation in Jesus? The answer was that it was the same God who had spoken in the past who was speaking in the present, but now the voice was clearer, the light brighter. Just as one can see the continuity between a preliminary sketch and the final painting, so we see the connection between past and present, but acknowledge the superiority of what happens in Christ. But the revelation of the past is not abandoned but recycled, and becomes a way of expressing what is happening in Christ. Christians take over all the claims made for the Law, all the symbols of Jewish religion, and use them for Christ: he is indeed the fulfilment of the Law.

Let us stay with the Fourth Gospel for a moment, and have another look at what is going on. In those first eighteen verses, which we know as the Prologue, the author sets out his conviction that it is the same divine Word which spoke at creation, in the Law, and through the Prophets, which is now embodied in Jesus. Some scholars believe that the author of the Fourth Gospel did not himself write this passage, but whether he did or not, he sets it at the beginning of his book, and clearly expects us to see it as the key to what follows. And what *does* follow? John's Gospel, as we all know, is structured on a series of miracles, or signs, interleaved with long discourses which spell out the significance of the signs. The very first of the signs is one I have already referred to – the changing of water into wine. The water had been intended for Jewish rites of purification; by changing it into wine, Jesus is said to manifest his glory. Immediately after this, Jesus goes to Jerusalem and drives out the money changers and the sacrificial animals from the temple. This, of course, is not itself a miracle, but Jesus is asked for a sign of his authority for acting in this way: 'Destroy this temple,' he declares, 'and in three days I will raise it again.' In these two scenes, therefore, John provides us with two symbols of the replacement of Judaism by the new life brought by Jesus. The water of purification is transformed into wine; the sacrifices in the temple give way to worship centred on a new temple – namely, the risen body of Christ. And just in case we have not seen the point, John spells it out for us in the discourse which follows, where a Jewish rabbi named Nicodemus is told that he must be born again, in order to enter the new world of God's kingdom. When Nicodemus fails to understand, Jesus expresses astonishment: a Jewish teacher should certainly have understood these things. The old must give way to the new, and any Jewish teacher worth his salt should, in John's eyes, have recognized what was going on. In fact, a Samaritan woman of dubious reputation – the very last person, you might think, to possess theological insight – proves to be much more perceptive than Nicodemus. It is true that they both make the same mistake by taking Jesus' words literally: 'Give me living water,' she begs Jesus, 'so that I don't have to come to the well.' She does not at first believe that Jesus is greater than Jacob who dug the well, but in the end not only she but a large number of Samaritans confess Jesus to be the saviour of the world. And what is the subject of the conversation between Jesus and the Samaritan woman? It is the proper place of worship. 'The time is coming,' says Jesus, 'when you will worship the Father, neither on this mountain nor in Jerusalem; God is Spirit, and those who worship must worship in spirit and in truth.' And immediately the subject of the conversation switches to the significance of Jesus himself – for as we know already, the temple which is to replace the one in Jerusalem is the temple of Christ's risen body: this is where his believers meet and worship God.

In this opening sequence of events, John sets the scene for the rest of his gospel: the old way of Judaism gives way to the new way of the gospel: purification rites, sacrifices, worship in the temple – all are transformed into a new spiritual worship centred on Jesus. In the chapters which follow, Jesus makes several journeys to Jerusalem – journeys not referred to in the other Gospels – at the time of the Jewish festivals, and a series of signs and discourses at these festivals demonstrate the significance of Jesus for his people. Many of the images which Jesus now applies to himself had been used in the past for the Law – but now, we discover, it is Jesus who is bread, life, light, the source of living water, the way, the truth. It is a gigantic take-over bid for everything that the Law had once signified – and for everything that the festivals had signified too, for many of the themes were linked with particular festivals, most notably bread at Passover. And linked with Passover also, of course, was the Passover lamb; that, too, seems to be lurking in John's mind. Right at the beginning of the Gospel, even before the wedding at Cana, he describes how John the Baptist picked out Jesus with the words 'Behold the lamb of God'. Johannine scholars are still debating what sort of lamb this might be, but a Passover lamb is one obvious possibility; certainly we discover, when we get to the end of the story, that on John's chronology Jesus dies at the very moment when the Passover lambs were being slaughtered in the temple. From now on there was no need for lambs to be slaughtered in the temple, since they had been replaced by God's own passover lamb. So the Fourth Evangelist traces continuity between old and new, and underlines the superiority of what happens in Christ, not only in relation to the Law, but in relation to Jewish worship also.

The theme of sacrifice dominates another New Testament book, the Epistle to the Hebrews, and we are shown there how Christ replaces all Jewish sacrifices. Whereas Paul is chiefly concerned with relating Christ to the Law (though he, too, refers to him as 'our Passover'), the author of Hebrews is concerned to relate Christ to the cult. Jesus not only replaces the sacrificial victims, however; he is also the great and perfect high priest who has offered the perfect sacrifice – himself. Logic protests that he cannot be both priest and victim, but of course the sheer illogicality of the picture is a good indication of what is going on: as we saw last time, it was not that there was a set programme which Jesus fulfilled: rather, Christians applied every image in the book that seemed in any way appropriate: every aspect of the Old Testament can be understood as pointing to Jesus, and it is a question of 'anything they can do, he can do better'. The two appear to be related as shadow to reality.

What was it that led the author of Hebrews to work out his faith in Jesus in these terms? The traditional answer has always been that he feared that his readers were in danger of

71

slipping back into Judaism. He warns them against this by demonstrating that the Jewish cult is out of date and ineffectual. If this is his position, then his attitude to the sacrificial system appears to be parallel to Paul's attitude to the Law and circumcision, seeing them as incompatible with faith in Christ. But wait a moment; Paul's concern is with Gentile Christians *accepting* the Law and circumsicion, and he never suggests that it is wrong for Jewish Christians to go on eating kosher meat, for example: only that they must not impose their way of life on others. Was it *wrong* for Jewish Christians to continue worshipping in the temple and offering sacrifices there? Did Luke totally misunderstand the situation when he depicted Paul hurrying to Jerusalem for Pentecost (Acts 20.16)? Have we perhaps once again misread the situation because we have interpreted it from a Gentile–Christian viewpoint? I have a suspicion that the problem behind this epistle may have been a somewhat different one from that which is normally supposed – not that the Hebrews, whoever they were, were in danger of slipping back into Judaism, but rather that they had been cut off from Jewish worship: perhaps (like those mentioned in John 9.22) they had been excommunicated from the Jewish synagogue, and this led our author to think about Christians in relation to Jewish worship; or perhaps they were Diaspora Jews, who rarely got to Jerusalem, but would rather like to: no need, our author assures them. Or perhaps – and this seems to me the most likely situation – the epistle was written after AD 70. The Jewish–Christian community is distressed at what has happened in Jerusalem, and more particularly at what has happened to the temple: no matter, our author tells them, for we Christians have no need of any further sacrifice. What need is there for candles, once you have been plugged into the mains? Perhaps then, the 'Hebrews' are not so much being warned not to slip

72

back into Judaism, as being urged to move *forwards*, out of it.

But we should be wrong to suppose that the author of Hebrews is presenting a totally *negative* view of the past: indeed, he traces continuity between past and present by claiming that Christ belongs to the order of Melchizedek. Just as *Paul* argues that what happens in Christ is the fulfilment of the covenant promises made to Abraham, and maintains that the Law was an interim measure, so the author of Hebrews traces Christ's pedigree back to Melchizedek, and claims that this priesthood was superior to that of the Levites, who came in between Melchizedek and Christ. Once again, the past points beyond itself, and so is revealed as temporary. The Jewish cult turns out to be an earthly copy of a heavenly original, now fully carried out through the death of Christ.

Notice the claims that are being made for Christ. It is not simply that he fulfils past promises, or that in him the Spirit of God is seen to be still at work: rather it is that in him God's *original* purposes are being worked out. The Law was never meant to save; the sacrifices were never intended to achieve lasting reconciliation between God and man. It is not simply that these things have worn out and need replacing, but that they were interim measures only. The word spoken at creation, the plan by which God created the universe, the covenant made with Abraham, the promises made to Abraham and to his descendants – all these are embodied in Christ. And *that* means that those who believe in Jesus have every right to claim that they belong to God's people: they may be newcomers, but they are not usurpers. For the author of Ephesians, it is not simply God's purpose for Christ that can be traced back to the creation, but his purpose for *us*: he offers praises to God who has 'chosen us in Christ before the foundation of the world'. Those who were once outsiders have been made 'fellow citizens with the saints' as God intended.

I suggested at the end of my last lecture that the first Christians had to wrestle with two questions of identity: who was Jesus? and who were *they*? I have found it impossible to deal with those two questions separately, and this is because they too, in answering the first, found themselves answering the second: the two questions belong together because Jesus and the community belong together. Affirmations about the status of Christ are echoed in affirmations about the status of those who believe in him. He is the Son of God – and they, in turn, become the children of God; he is the first-born from the dead – and they share in his resurrection; he is the promised king, who brings salvation to his people; he is Lord, and those who acknowledge his lordship share his rule; the engimatic phrase 'the Son of Man', whatever its origin, is understood to refer to Jesus, but again and again the evangelists insist that his followers will share in the suffering, vindication and authority of the Son of Man. Many of our New Testament images demonstrate how closely Jesus and those who believe in him are bound together: the church is the body of Christ, and Christians are members of that body; he is the tree, Christians the branches; the Christian community is a temple – of which Christ is the foundation stone; he is the shepherd of the sheep. But notice how those same affirmations and images bind together past and present: Jesus' death and resurrection are, we know, worked out in the experience of individual believers, who find the way to life through sharing in his death. But there is a sense in which they are worked out also in the history of God's people, for there, too, we see death and resurrection. Israel was called to be God's son, but through disobedience has lost the claim to that title; others have taken it over. Israel rejected God's Messiah, and so has been in turn rejected; but a new people of God has emerged. The one who joins past and present, old and new is the promised Davidic king – true inheritor of the promises, and true nucleus of the new community. The temple has been destroyed – but it is now rebuilt, as a sanctuary which is not made with hands; the tree has been cut down – but it has sprouted again, and new branches have been grafted in; the shepherd has been slain – but once again he is leading his flock. These images perhaps express better than anything else the relationship between continuity and discontinuity which we have been exploring. For though I have several times used the image of a take-over bid, it may be that this image is as misleading as that of the cuckoo. Certainly these early Christians would have rejected it. For what *they* were claiming was that they were real members of the family – adopted, maybe, but outsiders no longer; moreover, their inclusion in the family was no afterthought, but had been part of God's plan from the very beginning of time.

The tragedy, it seems to me, is that in the course of time the antagonism between Jew and Christian became so bitter that Christians began to behave like cuckoos, or like tycoons who had taken over the company. So concerned were they with their own position in God's scheme of salvation that they ceased to ask fundamental questions about God's purpose for 'Israel according to the flesh'. They forgot that poignant verse in Romans in which Paul declares: 'I could wish that I myself were accursed and cut off from Christ for the sake of my brothers, my kinsmen by race.' For by the time that the church had become a predominantly Gentile community, it had been cut off, not from Christ, but from Paul's kinsmen.

I have been attempting in these lectures to understand the situation of those who wrestled with the problems of relating old and new in the first years of the Christian era: if we wish to understand the origins of our faith, then clearly it is essential to explore the context in which it was first formulated. It may well be that the way in which these men and women related old and new may be of help to Christians today who experience the tension between past tradition and present experience. It may be that a better understanding of what was going on as the Christian community sought to establish its own identity could affect our attitudes to questions concerning Jewish–Christian relationships today. But these are questions for theologians rather than for the New Testament historian, and I must leave them to others to explore.